new start, new me!

Build the Foundations for Successful Weight Loss

© Weight Loss Resources 2016

Published by: Weight Loss Resources Ltd, 2C Flag Business Exchange, Vicarage Farm Road, Peterborough PE1 5TX.

Tel: 01733 345592

www.weightlossresources.co.uk

ISBN 978-1-904512-16-5

Printed and bound in the UK

PART 1:
Understand and Leverage Your Motivation

"Today, is the first blank page of your New Me Story. Write a Good One."

Hi,

I'm your New Me Book. The people who have written me are hoping that I can help you to lose weight successfully.

But, between friends, I need a bit of input to do that to the best of my ability.

Don't get me wrong, there is helpful, relevant and insightful information in this book – but nothing as interesting and relevant as you, and nothing as helpful as your own insight.

So, talk to me. Treat me as your secret friend. I can't speak and I won't judge, but if you pick up a pen and scribble your thoughts now and then, you'll get the best out of me.

With your help, this little book will give you a great start along the path of successful, long term, weight loss.

From getting yourself into the right frame of mind to the practical steps you can take to help yourself along.

- Find, understand and leverage your motivation
- Uncover the habits that lead you to gain weight
- Make changes that suit you and fit into your lifestyle
- Set goals for yourself

Be prepared to ask yourself some questions, do a bit of thinking, and even some daydreaming!

What's Your Attitude?

Research shows that one of the most important factors that influences weight loss success is your attitude towards it:

- Whether or not you believe that you can make the changes you need to make
- Whether or not you believe that the changes are worth making

Pretty much every one finds change challenging. So it makes sense to build up your reserves of motivation early on.

You need to go a bit deeper than the annual 'I'm going to lose weight' resolution.

So here's a couple of things worth exploring...

Your Weight Story Line

Draw a line on the graph showing the ups and downs of your weight over time.

Write your ages on the bottom scale going back as far as you think is relevant. Put an appropriate range of weights on the left-hand scale.

Jot down the main points of the story your line tells

_____

_____

_____

_____

new start · new me!

Highest								
Weight								
Lowest								

Then Age ____   **Mid Point** Age ____   **Now** Age ____

*"What you do today...
can improve all
your tomorrows!"*

What Sort of things Bother You Most About Your Weight Now?

Give it some thought, try to write at least one thing down here now

_____

_____

_____

_____

_____

_____

_____

_____

new . new
start me!

"What you get by achieving your goals is not as important as what you become by achieving your goals."

Jot Down Some Different Ways that Losing Weight Will Make a Difference to Your Life?

_____

_____

_____

_____

_____

_____

_____

_____

_____

_____

new . new
start me!

How Confident Are You That You Can Lose Weight?

Put a cross on the line where you think you are now. Ask yourself the questions opposite - important because they'll help you see potential problems and get ideas for solutions.

Why have you chosen that level and not a lower level?

_____

_____

_____

_____

What do you think it would take for you to move one notch up?

_____

_____

_____

_____

new . new
start ❤ me!

Give Your Confidence a Boost

We are all better at doing or being some things than we are at others.

Spending a bit of time recognising what you can do, or have achieved, can help you build confidence in other areas.

Some possible starting points for your thinking:

- Projects you have bought to successful completion, whether it's redecorating a room or landing a new job

- Times when you've made something happen

- Family you've nurtured, friends you've helped

    - Fears you've overcome to enable you to do things

Jot Down Your Highlights . . .

_____

_____

_____

_____

_____

_____

_____

_____

_____

new start new me!

"When you're doubting how far you can go, think about how far you have come."

PART 2:

Getting Started on Your Weight Loss Journey

You Want to Lose Weight – Where Do You Start?

From where you are now.

How aware are you of what you eat? And, more importantly for weight loss, how much energy is what you eat providing to your body? If it's more energy than you're actually using in a day, your body will store it as fat.

To our clever bodies, storing excess energy as fat makes a lot of sense – you wouldn't throw a litre of fuel away just because the car doesn't need it right now. You'd keep it in the garage for the day when there's a fuel strike.

The first problem is our bodies' lack of external storage, our extra fuel needs to stay in the boot – or the belly, thighs . . .

The next problem is the sheer number of opportunities to take in excess energy we're presented with.

In the last 50 years, the availability and convenience of food of all types has grown exponentially. Stacked high and sold cheap.

Much of this food is energy dense – lots of refined carbs, sugar and fat, processed beyond its ability to satisfy hunger.

But our bodies, clever as they are, take thousands more than 50 years to adapt to changes in our environment.

So, if you want to lose weight you have to take control, think about your choices. Stop letting your body save up for a fuel strike and find out, for yourself, what it really needs.

Find Out Where You Are

We'd strongly recommend that you keep, an ultra-honest, food diary for at least a few days before you even think about trying to change anything.

You may be quite surprised at what this shows you, even over a short period of time. Maybe...

- You didn't realise how many calories you were consuming overall or in certain foods or drinks

- You can immediately see that some specific food/drink habits you have are over-filling the fuel tank and could be relatively easy to change.

For example, the latte and Danish that's just supposed to be a mid-morning snack comes in at nearly 600 calories. Pretty much the same benefit could be achieved with a double espresso and a cereal bar for half the calories.

If you take that little scenario over the course of a year, you're talking about a difference of over half a stone in weight – and that's just one thing that keeping an honest food diary will help you reveal.

You might not like Danish pastries, or you may not drink coffee, but there will be elements of your day-to-day eating that will jump out at you. For a lot of us, it's what we do every day, without really thinking, that results in weight gain.

Here's What Some WLR Members Discovered

"I had no idea that I was eating a double portion of breakfast cereal every day."

"I thought that missing lunch would help my weight. But little snacks in the afternoon, plus being ravenous enough to need instant dinner when I got home from work were a disaster. Ravenous needs big dinner, early dinner means late night snacks... "

"I don't really know why, but if I have nice food in front of me, I am going to eat it until I'm so stuffed I feel bad – seconds if they are available. It's like, if I don't eat it all now, I'll be missing out."

"I don't know anyone who doesn't have a blowout sometimes, even my skinny friends who I am capable of hating when they complain about a little post meal bulge. But when you realise you're doing it pretty much every day... "

"I'm worried that my diet's not very healthy, so I drink quite a lot of fruit juice – couldn't believe how many calories in the amount I was drinking."

"I joined a gym on a route that passed a McDonalds. I went to the gym straight from work. Getting some protein after my workout (in the form of a burger meal) seemed like the obvious choice and a reward for my effort."

"*Knowing yourself is the beginning of all wisdom*"

What Do You Think Right Now?

If you decided to make changes, what might you focus on first?

_____

_____

_____

_____

_____

_____

_____

_____

new start me!

"We first make
our habits,
then our habits
make us."

PART 3:

Get to Know
Your Habits

The Habits We Have Tend to Make Some Kind of Sense

We brush our teeth because we want to keep them, go to work because we need the money, eat takeaway because we're busy and snacks because we're bored.

Habits help us quickly and easily navigate through daily routine without having to think about it very much.

But the very mindlessness that makes habits useful can work against us when it comes to what, why and when we eat.

The next few questions will help you identify areas where you may need to give your habits a bit of a makeover.   Score each question 0-3 points depending on how closely it resembles you.

My Habits 1

I eat a lot of snacks (eg chocolate, crisps, pastries, bars) because I don't have time for proper meals

Score _____

I have a very hectic schedule and tend to grab food on the go or choose quick to heat up meals

Score _____

I find it too much hassle to plan, and shop for, a healthy diet

Score _____

Total Score for My Habits 1 _____

My Habits 2

I continue to eat food even though I know that it's more than my body really needs

Score _____

When second helpings are available I'll have some

Score _____

When I choose, or am given, only a small meal or snack, I am worried that it won't be enough

Score _____

Total Score for My Habits 2 _____

My Habits 3

I use food to try and feel better if I am feeling low, stressed or bored

Score _____

I experience episodes when I can't seem to stop eating

Score _____

I eat to satisfy something other than hunger

Score _____

Total Score for My Habits 3 _____

What's the Score?

Your score for each set of habits will give you an idea of where to pay the most attention first. The higher the score, the more to be gained by delving a bit deeper into that area.

Don't worry if you have similar scores in two or three areas, it means you have lots of opportunity to tweak your habits and lose weight!

- Habits 1 indicates chaotic eating

- Habits 2 indicates portion size issues

- Habits 3 indicates emotional eating

Part 4 gives some pointers for working on these areas.

PART 4:
Line Up Your Targets

1. Make Order Out of Chaos
2. Get Portions in Proportion
3. Find Better Ways to Feel Better

Fail to Plan, Plan to Fail

If you think you've gained weight because your eating habits are all over the place. Here's some ideas on how you could get more control over the situation.

Planning meals and snacks can be one of the most helpful and effective things you can do when trying to lose weight.

Your lifestyle is probably the most important factor to take into account when you're creating a plan, get that part right and you'll be well on your way to success.

*"A goal
without a plan
is just a wish."*

Plan for Your Lifestyle

Think about your lifestyle. What sort of days do you have?

- On the run days

- At a desk days

- Going out tonight days

- Time off days

- Days out

- Family days

- Lunch date days

It's not a complete list but you get the idea. You probably have a combination of the above or some other type of days.

The important thing is recognising that you'll need a different plan for each type of day.

The next step is to think about all the times you normally eat on each type of day.

Then the fun starts. What foods could you fit in to each of your eating time slots?

If your goal is weight loss, you'll be looking for food you'll enjoy, that works in the particular situation, without overloading you with calories.

If you find yourself a bit short of ideas you can get loads of tasty but healthy meal and snack ideas accessible from the WLR food diary.

Plan for Your Health

Healthy eating is more than just a slogan.

As well as your weight, what you eat affects your

- quality of life

- how long you live

- how you look

- how you feel

There's no such thing as a healthy food, nor are single foods in isolation 'unhealthy'.

It's finding a good balance between all the foods that you eat that'll make your diet healthy.

Here's What the UK Health Department Recommends

- Fruit and Vegetables - at least 5 servings daily

- Bread, Other Cereals and Potatoes - 5 servings a day

- Milk and Dairy Foods - 2-3 servings daily

- Meat, Poultry, Fish, Eggs and Other Protein - 2-3 servings daily

- High Fat and/or High Sugar Foods - eat in small quantities, 0-3 servings daily

A good general rule is that food you prepare at home from basic ingredients (even when they are tinned or frozen ingredients) will be better for you than food that's made in a factory.

Plan for Your Calorie Needs

On average, women need around 2000 calories a day, men around 2500, to maintain weight within a healthy range.

If you want to lose weight. you'll have to eat less calories than your body needs to maintain its current weight:

- 500 calories less each day to lose a pound a week

- 1000 calories less each day to lose 2lbs a week

A diet of between 1100 and 1500 calories a day for women, and 1500-2000 calories a day for men, should produce a regular weight loss of 1 to 2lbs a week

You'll need to juggle the number of calories you eat and drink to fit how many you need to reach your weight loss goal.

If you're not a WLR member, A good calorie counter will make this easier – we recommend the Calorie Carb and Fat Bible 2016 as the most comprehensive.

Browsing through recipes, either online or in books, will help you generate some ideas.

If you feel you'd benefit from a bit more structure to start with, then maybe starting off with a basic, healthy diet plan would be a good idea. You'll find lots of these on the WLR website and you don't need to be a member to access them.

All of the plans in WLR enable you to swap things around so that you get meals that you like, that fit into your circumstances on the day.

Plan for a Little Bit of What You Fancy

Keep it real when you're planning your diet - cutting out all the foods, or drinks, you really enjoy will just make you feel deprived and resentful.

Make room for favourites, just have them in smaller portions, or less often, if they are high in calories. Here's some ideas:

- Drink a low calorie soft drink, or water, between alcoholic drinks on a night out

- Have a Happy Meal rather than a regular Meal Deal

- A handful of grapes is great for when you fancy something sweet

- Have a 25g bag of crisps rather than a 40g

Planning Tips

- Be specific - don't just tell yourself to eat less junk food in the evenings. Plan for proper, satisfying evening meals that will reduce the urge to snack

- Think about the upcoming week and decide what, where when you're going to eat.

- Prepare dinners when you have free time and freeze them to use when you're busy.

- If you're going to be out, at work or play, pack up a tasty and healthy lunch the night before

- Make a list of healthy foods and meals you like, find out how many calories in them, and plan accordingly.

"Planning is bringing the future into the present so that you can do something about it now."

What Days and/or Meals Do You Think You'd Most Benefit from Planning?

Jot down any ideas you have for plans as well!

_____

_____

_____

_____

_____

_____

_____

_____

new start new me!

Get Portions in Proportion

Over the last few decades portions have increased in size along with our expectations; we are bombarded with 'supersize' and 'all you can eat'.

Cheaply available food means what we perceive as a serving today can often be almost double what is was 20 years ago!

It's no wonder we're eating more than we realise – the lovely picture of a bowl of cereal on the pack could be up to 100g; yet the actual per serving nutrition info is for only 30-40g!

How can you start to control your portions? Change always starts with seeing where you are right now, so take a look at how big your portions really are.

Most people are surprised when they start to weigh what they 'normally' have and look at the number of calories it contains.

You might find that you're dishing up substantially more than you think!

Dietitian Juliette Kellow says

"The problem is that when we are presented with more food on a plate than will meet our needs, most of us will eat more without even thinking about it.

The good news is that studies showing we eat more calories when given more, also show that we still feel satisfied when given less."

Smaller Portions Don't Mean You'll Be Hungry

In one study, the size of a pasta dish portion served was varied between a standard serving and a serving 50% larger.

Customers who ordered the meal were asked to rate their satisfaction and the appropriateness of the portion size.

The results showed that customers who were served the larger portion ate nearly all of it - consuming an extra 172 calories.

The interesting thing is that responses to a post-meal survey showed that customers rated the size of both portions as equally satisfying.

Go figure...

It seems we're losing touch with what it means to eat as much as our bodies need, and the food environment we're in is making us fat.

Eating out is especially difficult. Many restaurants serve portions that are far too big for most people, but leaving food on a plate can be quite hard to do – even when we know there's really too much.

Whilst waiting for the food industry to change, those of us who want to be a healthy weight need to take control of our own portion sizes.

Deciding to eat food in amounts that our bodies really need is a good starting point.

Making Changes to Your Portion Sizes

- Weigh foods so you get to know what a quantity of food looks like and how many calories are in it

- Slow Down – take smaller bites and put your knife and fork down between mouthfuls

- Bulk meals out with veggies and salads

- Use a smaller plate

- Enjoy and savour your food so you're paying attention and know when you're starting to feel full

- Stop eating as soon as you think you've had 'sufficient'. Don't worry about being hungry later, you probably won't be, and anyway you can eat something if you really are.

A Portion of Fun

Estimate what you think the weight of your 'normal' portions of these foods are. (Check how close your estimates were by weighing the foods next time you're going to eat them.)

Your favourite breakfast cereal   _____

Your serving of pasta   _____

Your glass of fruit juice   _____

Your serving of rice   _____

Your portion of chips   _____

Your piece(s) of pizza   _____

The Illusion of Food Making Us Feel Better

Nearly 60% of women who want to lose weight, and over 30% of men, report eating in response to how they are feeling emotionally rather than because they are actually hungry.

Food becomes a way to deal with emotions. Stress, boredom, loneliness, sadness, disappointment or other negative emotions can be temporarily pushed to one side with some comforting food or drink.

This can be a real hurdle when it comes to losing weight. As well as the excess calories eaten, we're often left feeling worse because on top of the negative emotion we now have to contend with feeling bad because we've eaten too much.

Understand Why You Eat

If you ever find yourself rummaging in the fridge even though you've recently eaten, then you know hunger isn't the reason.

More than likely some negative emotion has triggered a habit of using food to feel better.

The urge to eat can be so automatic that you feel you lack willpower or are out of control. But it is in fact a learned or conditioned response.

Because this 'non-hungry' eating is learned, it is possible to re-programme your response to the situations or feelings that trigger it.

Increase Your Awareness

The first step is to identify when these urges strike. When you find yourself at the fridge when you aren't hungry, ask yourself 'why do I want to eat? What am I feeling?'

If you aren't sure, think back to what was happening before you felt the urge. Then ask yourself if there is another way you can feel better.

Or you could 'chat' to your urge to eat - telling it that you aren't actually hungry, it isn't actually going to help, and it's nothing more than a conditioned response.

Whatever strategy you choose, the more often you break the 'eating when you're not hungry' habit, the weaker its hold.

How's Your Self-Talk?

When you look in the mirror do you talk to yourself more like A or B?

A 'I'll never be slim. I've only lost a measly couple of pounds in four weeks. And I broke my diet last night, I may as well just give up.'

B 'This is going well, those few pounds have really made a difference. I enjoyed a treat last night, now I'm really looking forward to watching the next half a stone disappear.'

Both of these examples of 'self-talk' (automatic thoughts, or statements all of us constantly make to ourselves) will have an effect on how we feel and act.

Self-talk may be positive and constructive (like your guardian angel) or negative and irrational (like having a destructive devil on your shoulder).

If you've had on-off battles with your weight over the years, it's highly likely that the 'devil' is there more often.

Self-talk that says 'you're hopeless', can make you feel like a failure which can then trigger you into the action of overeating and/or totally giving up trying to lose weight.

One of the most powerful things about self-talk is that the last thoughts we have are what stays in our mind. So whether we think 'I still look fat' or 'wow, I'm really getting slimmer' will stay with us until we think again.

Practise Positive Self-Talk

The trick is to listen out for your self-talk and catch it as it's happening.

Then turn negative self-talk into positive – like in the example above where A and B see the same events in a completely different light.

Try talking to yourself like you'd speak to your best friend!

Reshaping negative self-talk helps you to change the way you see yourself - from 'someone who can't' lose weight, or achieve what they want, to 'someone who can'.

And when you believe you can... you can.

Really Choose What You Want to Eat

This strategy is like your personal brake. It also helps you manage 'non-hungry' eating and weaken its hold.

It legalises food, makes eating a positive choice and stops you feeling deprived.

It also helps you to regularly remind yourself why you are making changes to your eating habits, which keeps your motivation to lose weight high.

But it doesn't just happen. Like all skills it requires practise.

Practise Consciously Choosing

Before you eat anything, ask yourself if you really want the food in front of you.

This becomes the prompt for you to make a conscious choice, weighing up the pros and cons of making that choice, and feeling free to have it, reject it or just eat some.

Remembering all the while that you can eat this food another time if you want to.

Paul's story on the next page is a good example of how empowering this technique is when you put it into practice.

Paul's Story

Paul is having a business lunch at a restaurant he visits regularly. His favourite dish is steak béarnaise and fries then crème caramel.

But at his last medical his doctor advised him to lose weight for his heart's sake. He has taken this seriously and thought a lot about changing his lifestyle.

But he can't avoid business lunches.

Faced with the menu Paul's automatic response is the steak and chips.

But then he stops and thinks.

- How hungry is he?

- How will he feel after he eats it?

- What would be a better and still tasty choice?

After all he comes here quite a bit, so can order the steak another time.

He opts for a spicy chicken fillet with new potatoes and vegetables. He really enjoys the spicy flavour, and feels comfortably satisfied, rather than stuffed and guilty.

Paul feels great – he's has made a good choice for himself that he really enjoyed, which boosts his confidence.

Take it Step by Step

Learning new habits and ways of thinking about things takes time.

Think back to when you learned to drive a car.

You didn't expect yourself to pass your test after half a dozen lessons.

There were probably times when you thought that all the things you have to remember to do when you're driving would never come naturally to you.

Step by step, you took control of the car and learned how to keep it on course. Just like you can do with your weight.

Take it Seriously

It's really worth spending a bit of time on this, when it all 'clicks' good things happen...

- Mental blocks ebb away

- Motivations become clear and powerful

- Your self-worth and belief in your abilities grow

- You take control by making real choices - knowing and accepting the consequences – and no longer feeling deprived.

- You move from being someone who can't lose weight long term, to being someone who can.

"For me, my mood can have a direct effect on my eating habits; my responses can be triggered by emotion and when I am down or despondent I can find myself reaching for food or drink in the hope that it will raise my spirits."

What Kinds of Feelings, Moods, Problems or Events Can Lead You to Reach for Food?

_____

_____

_____

_____

_____

_____

_____

_____

_____

new start ❤ new me!

"Each of us is on a unique journey... we all face different challenges... we all have different 'highs' and 'lows'; we all respond differently to external (and internal) factors. There is no right or wrong... but there is always choice. We can choose to see things in a bleak light or in a brighter context..."

What Kinds of Things Could You Do to Cheer Yourself Up, Chill Out, or Re-Energise Without Reaching for Food or Drink?

_____

_____

_____

_____

_____

_____

_____

_____

new start . new me!

*"Let exercise
be your stress reliever,
not food"*

PART 5

What About Exercise?

*"Fitness is not about being better than someone else...
It's about being better than you used to be."*

Do I Need to Exercise?

Strictly speaking exercise is not necessary for weight loss.

It will, however

- Make weight loss easier
- Conserve muscle (muscle burns more calories)
- Mean you can eat a bit more and still lose weight
- Raise your level of motivation (quite a lot)
- Give a nicer shape to your body
- Help keep your bones strong
- Help you live a better quality of life, and for longer

Getting More Active

Building up your activity levels, even just a little, can really help when you're trying to lose weight.

Many WLR members discover that getting some exercise makes it easier to lose weight, and boosts confidence and self- esteem.

You burn more calories, you feel good, you're more motivated.

Getting started with exercise doesn't need to be overwhelming, and any activity you do can make a difference.

If you struggle to do much exercise activity at all, setting a realistic and achievable goal of say 10 minutes a day, or even every other day, would be a great start.

This activity could be going for a brisk walk or bike ride, or doing something simple at home like putting on some music and having a good dance around the house.

Anything that feels like exercise to you will do.

If you spend most of your time indoors, try to do something outside, the fresh air almost doubles the energy enhancing effects of exercise.

"I've been doing a bit of bouncing on my little trampoline. I recorded a weekend radio show that plays 'Club Classics' and now have a four-hour playlist of some cracking disco tracks which put a smile on my face and assist with the spring in my step(s) as I jog and 'boing' merrily whilst singing loudly (and out of tune)."

What Kinds of Activities Might You Enjoy?

_____

_____

_____

_____

_____

_____

_____

_____

_____

_____

new new
start me!

"Breaking old habits and forming new ones takes time and effort, but you're worth it."

PART 6:

Over to You

Your New Start New Me Project

The following pages will help you to set up a simple action plan that will help you to organise your thoughts, set some goals and keep you on the track to success.

Your Confidence Number is the number where you put yourself on the chart on page 14 on the date you are taking measurements.

Your Feel-Good Number is your own marks out of ten for how good you're feeling about your progression.

Vital Statistics

The main reason these stats are vital is because they enable you to track progress in different ways. Seeing and recording progress puts your achievements to work for you.

	Date	Date	Date
Weight	____	____	____
Body Mass Index	____	____	____
Clothes Size	____	____	____
Confidence Number	____	____	____
Feel-Good Number	____	____	____

The Reasons I Want to Lose Weight Are

_____

_____

_____

_____

_____

_____

_____

_____

_____

new
start
new
me!

Losing Weight Will Benefit Me Because:

_____

_____

_____

_____

_____

_____

_____

_____

_____

new new
start me!

Three Changes I'm Going to Make to My Eating/Activity Habits:

1 _____

_____

_____

2 _____

_____

_____

3 _____

_____

_____

_____

new new
start me!

This is What I will Do if it Starts to Get Difficult, or I Come Up Against Obstacles:

_____

_____

_____

_____

_____

_____

_____

_____

_____

new new
start me!

My Weight Goals for the Next

Week:

_____

_____

_____

Month:

_____

_____

_____

Three Months:

_____

_____

_____

6 Months:

_____

_____

_____

We'd like to wish you the best of luck, health and feel-good factor.

new new
start me!

Need Some Help?

The infamous Weight Loss Resources Helpteam are on hand seven days a week. You just have to give them a call, send them an email or message, to get a prompt, understanding and helpful response.

Email helpteam@weightlossresources.co.uk

Phone 01733 345592

Or log in to the message boards at Weight Loss Resources. Post on the Helpteam message board or send us a private message.

Acknowledgements

This book doesn't have a single author. It's the result of the expertise and experience of Weight Loss Resources staff, members, dietitians and exercise professionals, past and present.

Here are the main contributors, thanks to them all.

Judith Carpenter BSc RD   Consultant Dietitian and Motivation Specialist
Lyndel Costain BSc RD   Consultant Dietitian
hudson14   WLR Blogger
Juliette Kellow BSc RD   Consultant Dietitian
Joanne Putney   WLR Designer
Carla van Traa REPS L4   Consultant Personal Trainer
Rebecca Walton   WLR Director
Tracey Walton   WLR Founder and MD